I0789679

TAPERSTARY

OF MY LIFE IN

RYME

My name is Terence Joseph Goodchild I was born in Manchester in the UK, at the age of nine years old I was put in an orphanage named St Josephs convent orphanage in Salford with my brother who was 6, we stayed in there for about two years and when we were released we were total wrecks, and all through my life I had to put up with having a stammer, being picked on laughed at and many other indignant things, at 16 I contemplated suicide by driving my car into the motorway bridge, but just as I was about to do the deed I stopped myself and thought there has to be a better way, and from that day onwards I became successful in my own right, and married a wonderful person, we have been together 53 years and married 50, and live on our farm in Tasmania Australia with our horses and a cat

and dog I have written 14 books about my life and where all the
people in the stories are part of me and my life

<u>ST JOSEPHS</u>

ST JOSEPHS CONVENT I HAVE SEEN

ST JOSEPHS CONVENT I HAVE BEEN

THE DARKENED HALL THE DARKENED PLACES

OF FRIEGHTENED CHILDREN WITH FRIGHTENED FACES

NEVER TOLD THE SPOKEN TRUTH

WHY I WAS PRISONED INSIDE THIS ROOF

I NEVER KNEW THE REASON WHY

WHY THEY TOOK IT WITH THEM WHEN THEY DIE

THOSE HALLOWED HALLS AS SEEN THE LAST

OFF ME AND MINE AND ALL MY PAST

THE TRUTH ONE DAY I WILL FIND

THOUGH IT TAKES THOUGHT AND IT TAKES TIME

I KNOW THE TRUTH THAT YOU HOLD DOWN

I EVERY DAY I WORE A FROWN

AND I WAS NEVER TOLD

WHY I WAS KEPT OUT IN THE COLD

WHAT IS THIS TRUTH YOU HOLD INSIDE

YOU TOOK MY HOPES YOU TOOK MY PRIDE

THEN ONE DAY I WAS LET OUT

AND I NEVER GAVE A SHOUT

FOR I HAD LEARNDED TO GROW UP FAST

AND THEN MY LIFE THE DIE IS CAST

THE POET

WHERE HAVE YOU COME FROM THE POET IN ME

ARE YOU FROM SOMEWHERE SOMEWERE I CANNOT SEE

FOR I DONT KNOW WHAT'S BRINGING THE WORDS OUT
IN RYME

ARE YOU FROM SOMEWHERE ELSE BACK IN TIME

ALL I WISH FOR IS SOME KIND OF SIGN

THAT MAKE ALL MY FEELINGS COME OUT IN RYME

ARE YOU A PERSON THAT TIME HAS FORGOT

THAT YOU WERE A POET AND I WAS NOT

AND THIS IS THE ONLY WAY YOU CAN FEEL

AND MAKE YOUR PRESENCE HERE REALLY REAL

I DONT UNDERSTAND WHY YOU CHOOSE THIS TIME

TO MAKE ALL MY FEELINGS COME OUT IN RYME

PERHAPS YOU ARE LONELY AND NEEDED SOMEONE

THAT YOU COULD TRUST AND RELAY UPON

AND MAKE ALL YOUR FEELINGS COME OUT IN RYME

FOR NOW IS THE HOUR AND NOW IS THE TIME

I REMEMBER

I REMBER WHEN I WAS YOUNG

I NEVER USED TO CRY

I NEVER USED TO LAUGH I NEVER USED TO SIGH

WHAT MAKES A PERSON DOES THESE THINGS

WHEN HE IS GROWING OLD

AND NEVER KNOWING WHAT TO SEE

AND ONLY KNOWING WHAT HE'S TOLD

FOR IF HE DID HIMSELF TO FIND

THE GREATEST GIFT TO ALL MANKIND

TO LOVE HIMSELF AND DEEP WITHIN

TO FIND THE LOVE AND NOT THE SIN

AND FIND THE THINGS THAT MAKE HIM WHOLE

THEN THE STORY HAS BEEN TOLD

<u>*MY STUTTER*</u>

WHAT LOOKS YOU GIVE ME WHAT WORDS YOU UTTER

WHEN YOU FIND I HAVE A STUTTER

YOU LOOK AT ME AS IF IM CURSED

YOU LOOK AT ME AND EVEN WORSE

YOU THINK IM DAFT YOU THINK IM LOONY

YOU THINK IVE JUST COME DOWN FROM THE MOONY

WHY DO YOU LAUGH WHY CANRN'T YOU SEE

THE PERSON WHO'S INSIDE OF ME

I LOVE I LAUGH I HURT I CRY

AND ONE DAY I WILL DIE

DONT YOU THINK I DESERVE A CHANCE

TO GROW TO LIVE AND TO ADVANCE

WHY CARN'T YOU UNDERSTAND IN ME

FOR I AM HERE FOR ALL TO SEE

BUT YOU KEEP ME IN A PRISON

AND MY SOUL HAS NEVER RISEN

TO THE HIEGHTS THAT YOU FEEL

FULL OF LIFE AND FULL OF ZEAL

I HAVE THIS TROUBLE WITH MY TALKING

BUT YOU STAND THERE BLOODY GALKING

IT'S NOT CONTAGIOUS YOU WONT CATCH IT

ON THE SURFACE YOU CARN'T SCRATCHED IT

SO WHEN THE REASON I DO TALK

AND YOU JUST STAND AND GALK

IT'S JUST ME THAT'S STANDING THERE

AND IM JUST HUMAN AS YOU SEE

I DIDN'T CHOOSE IT, IT CHOSE ME

SO STOP THE WAY YOU ARE TREATING ME

I AM JUST LIKE YOU AS YOU SEE

MY CHILDHOOD

MY CHILDHOOD DREAMS WHERE CAN THEY BE

MY CHILDHOOD DREAMS WHY CAN I NOT SEE

WHAT IS THIS BLOCK I FEEL INSIDE

THAT MAKES ALL MY THOUGHTS RUN AND HIDE

WHAT IS THE BLOCK I FEEL INSIDE

THAT MAKE ALL MY THOUGHTS RUN AND HIDE

WHY CAN I NOT SEE WHY CAN I NOT FEEL

IS IT MY FAULT YOU RUN AND HIDE

THROUGH BITTER THOUGHTS AND BITTER PRIDE

WHY CAN YOU NOT COME RIGHT OUT AND SEE

THE PERSON THAT IS REALLY ME

I WILL NOT BITE I WILL NOT SCRATCH

AND MAYBE WE BOTH CAN BE ATTACHED

TO OURSELVES AND BE AS ONE

AND ALL THE BAD MEMORIES WILL SOON BE GONE

<u>DREAMS AND HOPES</u>

WHAT THOUGHTS AND PLEASURES DO WE DERIVE

JUST FROM MEARLY BEING ALIVE

WHAT DREAMS AND HOPES WE HAVE ALL HIDDEN

FOR WANT'S AND POSSESSIONS WE ARE DRIVEN

WHAT OF THE DREAMS WE HAVE FORGOT

WE THROW ASIDE BECAUSE IT WAS NOT

THE THING TO DO TILL TIME FORGOT

WE HAVE CHOICES THAT I KNOW

THE THINGS WE WANT THE THINGS WE SHOW

BUT NOW'S THE TIME TO MAKE A STAND

AND TAKE YOUR FUTURE BY THE HAND

WE MUST BELIVE THAT WHAT IS RIGHT

AND MAKE THE DARKNESS INTO LIGHT

GO FOR DREAMS AND MAKE THEM HAPPEN

WE HAVE HELD BACK WE HAVE BEEN SLACKIN

NOW IS THE TIME FOU US TO GO

TO OURSELVES WE HAVE TO SHOW

<u>*OURSLEVES*</u>

FOR OURSELVES WE DO DECIVE

FOR OURSELVES WE DONT BELIVE

HIDDNE THOUGHTS AND HIDDEN DREAMS

HIDDEN SHOUTS AND HIDDEN SCREAMS

NEVER KNOWING DAY BE DAY

WHY WE RELLY ARE THIS WAY

PERHAPS ONE DAY I WILL TURN

THEN THE THOUGHTS I WILL REALLY SPURN

THEN WHEN THE LIGHT COMES RIGHT THROUGH

THEN TO MYSELF I WILL BE TRUE

WE HAVE A REASON TO TAKE FLIGHT

WHAT GIVES ME WORRY WHAT GIVES ME FRIGHT

WHAT MAKES ME THINK I CAN NOT COPE

WE LOOSE ALL REASON LOOSE ALL HOPE

FOR ALL THE THINGS I TRIED TO HIDE

THAT CAUSES TURMOIL AND FEAR INSIDE

WHAT HOPE HAVE I TO LIVE A LIE

FREE FROM WORRY FREE FROM STRIFE

WHAT IS THIS THING I CAN NOT FACE

THE THING THAT HAPPENS IN THIS PLACE

DOWN INSIDE MY SOUL IT HIDES

DEEP DOWN IT RESIDES

NOT EVER COMING TO THE LIGHT

PERHAPS ITS LIKE ME AND FULL OF FRIGHT

I FEEL INSIDE

YESTERDAY I FELT SAD

MY FEAR AND TRAUMA I CAN NOT HIDE

I NEED TO GO INSIDE MY SOUL

TO MAKE ME FILLED TO MAKE ME WHOLE

I FELT REJECTED, NEGLECTED AND STUPID

I NEED SOMEONE WITH THE ARROW OF CUPID

TO PIERCE THE DARKNESS I FEEL INSIDE

NO LONGER FOR MY FEARS TO HIDE

WHAT DO I WANT WHAT DO I FEAR

TO ME IT IS NOT REALLY CLEAR

WHY I RUN I HIDE I FEAR

I CAN NOT TELL I CAN NOT HEAR

LAST NIGHT AS I LAY IN MY BED

ALL THESE THOUGHTS RAN THROUGH MY HEAD

WHAT IS THIS THING THAT IS WELL HIDDEN

TO MAKE ME SAD TO MAKE ME DRIVEN

THAT CAUSES ALL THIS FEARFUL DREAD

THIS PAIN AND TORTURE IN MY HEAD

THIS DEMON THAT I CAN NOT TOUCH

THAT IS USING ME FOR HIS CRUTCH

ONE I WILL DRIVE IT OUT

THEN I WILL BE ABLE TO SHOUT

GLORY BE I AM FREE

THING TO PASS

I WON'T THIS THING I HAVE TO PASS

I WANT TO KICK IT IN TH ARSE

I HAVE HAD IT FOR SO LONG YOU SEE

THE DARKNESS THAT'S INSIDE OF ME

TO PLUCK IT FROM WHENCE IT HIDES

WHERE IT IS HIDDEN FROM WHERE IT RESIDES

ALL THE TRUTH I WILL SEE

WHAT IS THIS FEAR INSIDE OF ME

WHY DO I ALWAYS STAND AND WAIT

WHY CAN I NOT OPEN UP THE GATE

TO FIND WHAT IT IS I HATE

TO GO RIGHT IN AND NOT PROCRASTINATE

SO NOW I HAVE TO MAKE A STAND

AND OFFER OUT MY LOVING HAND

THEN ALL THE FEARS AND ALL THE DREAD

AND ALL THE THOUGHTS WITHIN MY HEAD

WILL ONE DAY SPREAD THEIR WINGS AND FLY

THEN MY LIFE WONT BE A LIE

<ins>*TIME TO FIGHT*</ins>

NOW IS THE TIME FOR ME TO FIGHT

TO GET IT OUT AND NOT TAKE FLIGHT

TO FACE THE HORROR THAT'S WITHIN

SO I CAN START ALL OVER AGAIN

I HAVE TO FACE WHAT I AM LEARNING

TO FIND THE TRUTH THAT I AM YEARNING

THE TRUTH IS THERE FOR ME TO SEE

TO MAKE MYSELF WHOLE AND FREE

IT TAKES TIME IF TAKES COURAGE

SO I MUST NOT BE DISCOURAGED

TO GO WHERE ANGELS FEAR TO TREAD

TO FACE THIS HURT TO FACE THIS DREAD

<u>**SHOWING ME**</u>

YOU SHOW ME THINGS THAT I DONT KNOW

YOU TAKE ME PLACES I DONT GO

YOU START TO TELL ME THEN LEAVE ME FLAT

YOU STAY THERE AND I GO BACK

WHAT IS THIS THING YOU TRY TO TELL

AND ALL THE WORDS YOU TRY TO SPELL

TO UNDERSTAND ME I MUST KNOW

TO UNDERSTAND ME I MUST GO

INTO THE PLACE YOU'R LEADING ME

TO SHOW YOU THINGS I HAVE TO SEE

DONT BE AFRAID BECAUSE I WON'T CRY

IVE DONE ALL THAT MY EYES ARE DRY

ILL SEE THE TRUTH THAT YOU WILL SHOW

YOU LEAD THE WAY I WANT TO GO

SO TAKE ME THERE WHERE I BELONG

FOR I HAVE WAITED FAR TO LONG

WITH YOU BESIDE ME I WON'T FALTER

THE TWO OF US MY LIFE WILL ALTER

THE TRUTH IS THERE FOR US TO FIND

SO TAKE ME THERE FOR IM NOT BLIND

WORDS

WORDS OF WISDOM COME TO US

SOME ARE NEGATIVE SOME ARE PLUS

IN OUR HANDS OUR LIVES UNFOLD

TO TRUTHS AND STORIES NEVER TOLD

WHAT ARE THESE THINGS THAT MAKE US WEEP

AND MAKE OUR MINDS THAT WE CARN'T SLEEP

AND ALL WE WISH FOR IS THE LIGHT

FOR DARKNESS BRINGS THE FEAR AND FRIGHT

AND WITH NOW SLEEP OUR MINDS STRUGGLE

OUR DAYS ARE WEARY FULL OF TROUBLE

WHAT IS OUR FEAR THAT MAKES US WAKEN

AND MAKES ARE BODIES TIRIED AND SHAKEN

FOR OUR FEAR INSIDE OUR MIND

AND IT'S BEEN THERE ALL THIS TIME

WILL IT COME OUT AND SHOW IT'S FACE

THEN WE'LL KNOW WEVE WON THE RACE

<u>**SEASONS**</u>

SEASONS COME AND SEASONS GO

IT'S DARK IN HERE SO I DONT KNOW

IF WRONG IS WRONG AND RIGHT IS RIGHT

WHY DONT YOU LISTEN TO MY PLIGHT

PLEASE FREE ME FROM WHERE I AM KEPT

AND THEN THE TRUTH I WILL EXCEPT

BUT I AM HELD IN THIS PLACE

AND YOU HAVE NEVER SEEN MY FACE

BUT WAIT ONE DAY I WILL BE THERE

AND OUT LIFE WE BOTH CAN SHARE

I JUST HOPE IT'S NOT TO LATE

FOR YOU TO OPEN UP THE GATE

I AM TRAPPEDWITHIN MY SOUL

AND ALL I WANT IS TO BE WHOLE

SO TRY YOUR BEST I KNOW YOU CAN

AND FREE ME FROM THE PLACE I AM

LOCKED IN SIDE

WHAT IS THIS FEAR THAT'S LOCKED INSIDE

WHY DONT YOU COME OUT YOU HAVEN'T TO HIDE

THERE'S NO ONE HERE TO CHASTISE YOU

YOU CAN BE HERE YOU CAN BE YOU

FOR WHAT'S THIS THING YOU FEEL AFRAID

THERE'S NOTHING WRONG YOU CAN BE BRAVE

AND LET GO OF ALL YOU FEEL

THE PAIN INSIDE WILL SURELY HEAL

NO NEED TO SHUT OUT SOMEONE CLOSE

WHO FEELS YOUR HURT WHO FEELS THE MOST

OF WHAT YOUVE BEEN THROUGH IN YOUR PAST

AND EARLY ON THE DIE WAS CAST

FOR NOW YOU ARE FREE TO BE YOURSELF

AND BE REBORN AND FULL OF WEALTH

STAMMER

MY STAMMERS WORSE MY SLEEPING IS BAD

WHY DO I FEEL THIS WAY

I USED TO FEEL A BETTER WAY

BUT THAT WAS JUST A LIE

AND NOW I FEEL DESPERATION CREEPING UP MY SPINE

I THINK IT'S TIME THAT YOU CAME OUT

AND GAVE ME A GOOD SIGN

THAT ALL THIS HURT AND FEAR

WILL AL ONE DAY DISAPEAR

AND LET ME LIVE MY LIFE ANEW

BUT DONT YOU HESTITATE FROM WHERE YOU ARE

AND WHY YOUVE HUNG AROUND

I WILL NOT BUDGE I WILL NOT FEAR

FOR I WILL STAND MY GROUND

I WANT TO KNOW JUST WHO YOU ARE

AND WHY YOUVE HUNG AROUND

AND MADE MY LIFE A HELL ON EARTH

AND LEFT ME UNDERGROUND

YOU HIDE IN SHADOWS DARK AND DAMP

AND NEVER SEE THE LIGHT

BUT NOW YOU JUST PISS ME OFF

BECAUSE YOU ARE FULL OF SHITE

SO SHOW YOURSELF IF YOU DARE

AND FACE ME FACE TO FACE

SO I CAN GET RID OF YOU

AND BLOW YOU FROM THIS PLACE

<u>DESPERATE FEELINGS</u>

DESPERATE FEELINGS WASH OVER ME

DESPERATE FEELINGS I CAN NOT SEE

I REALISE I AM VUNARABLE IVE NEVER FELT BEFORE

SOMETHING STRANGE IS COMING AND KNOCKING ON
MY DOOR

WHY CANRN'T THIS FEELING GO AWAY

AND LEAVE ME TO MYSELF

THEN I CAN BE SET FREE

FROM ALL MY TORMENT I HAVE LIVED FOR ALL THIS
TIME

WHY CAN IT NOT SHOW ITSELF AND GIVE ME A SIGN

I AM HERE I AM ME WHY DONT YOU SHOW YOURSELF

THEN WE CAN BOTH BE FREE

EVERYDAY I CLOSER COME BUT NOTHING SPRINGS TO
MIND

IF ALL MY FEELINGS FEEL THIS WAY

I THINK ITS NOW THE TIME

SO COME RIGHT OUT AND DO YOUR WORSE

THEN I CAN GET RID OF THIS CURSE

FOR CURSE IT IS AND CURSE IT BE

TO RID MYSELF AND BE SET FREE

IF FREEDOM IS THE PRICE I HAVE TO PAY

THEN DO YOUR WORSE I WANT TO PAY

SELDOM

SELDOM DO WE GET THE CHANCE

TO LIVE OUR LIFE AND TO ADVANCE

FOR MANY YEARS I HAVE THOUGHT ABOUT OTHERS

MOTHER FATHER SISTER BROTHER

BUT I AM HERE AND THEY ARE THERE

OUR LIVES MY CROSS BUT NEVER SHARE

THE GRUDGE I BORE JUST MADE ME ILL

I GOT THE ANSWER JUST A PILL

BUT NOW I KNOW THE ANSWERS THERE

FOR I KNOW AND THEY DONT CARE

THEY LIVE THIER LIVES INSIDE A SHELL

THE TRUTH IS THERE BUT THEY WONT TELL

BUT NOW I KNOW I AM TRULY RISEN

FOR THIER FALLINGS IVE FOGIVEN

BUT IF THEY DONT SEE AND THEY DONT TELL

IVE JUST THREE WORDS GO TO HELL

<u>GAZE OUTSIDE</u>

WHEN I LOOK AT GAZE OUTSIDE

IT FILLS MY HEART WITH WONDER AND PRIDE

AT TREES AND PLANTS AND GRASS AND THINGS

AT ANTS AND WORMS AND BIRDS THAT SING

TO MAKE THIS WORLD A BETTER PLACE GIVEN FREELY
TO OUR RACE

BUT WE FREELY DO ABUSE THE THINGS WE ARE GIVEN
FOR TO USE

WE MAKE THE RIVERS GREEN AND BLUE

AND MAKE THE FRESS AIR SMELL LIKE POO

AND WHEN WE LOOK AT WHAT WE ACHIEVE

WHO WILL CARE AND WHO WILL GRIEVE

FOR WHAT WE TRULY PUT ASUNDER

AND WHAT WE HUMAN RACE WILL PLUNDER

THE ACID RAIN THE DRIED UP LAKES

IS ALL WE ARE LEAVING IN OUR WAKE

AND WHAT IF CHILDREN NOT YET BORN

THEY WILL LOOK AND THEY WILL SCORN

FOR LEAVING NOTHING FOR THIER GAZE

AND ALL THE WONDERS TO AMAZE

WE HAVE GIVEN THEM TO LEARN

TO TAKE WHAT YOU WANT THE REST TO SPURN

LEAVING NOTHING FOR TO GENERATE

TO TAKE BY FORCE BY RAPE AND HATE

WE HAVENT TAUGHT THEM TO BE KIND AND TRUE

TO LEAVE SOMETHING FOR OTHERS TO VIEW

AND LEAVE THE WORLD A BETTER PLACE

FOR OTHERS OF THE HUMAN RACE

SOMEONE

TRAPPED INSIDE THIS MORTAL SOUL

IS THIS PERSON THAT IS WHOLE

THE MAN WHO IS TRYING TO BE ME

SOMEONE WHO WANTS SOMEONE TO SEE

HOW HE'S COPED FOR ALL THESE YEARS

THROUGH MANY LIES AND MANY TEARS

SOMEONE WHO WANTS THIS HURT TO GO

AND WANTS THE WORLD AROUND TO KNOW

THAT HE IS TRUE THAT HE IS STRAIGHT

AND AT THE GATE HE SLOWLY WAITS

FOR THIS PERSON TO SET HIM FREE

FOR ALL THIS HURT TO LET HIM SEE

THAT LIFE IS FULL OF LOVE AND WONDER

AND NOT OF HATE OR WAR AND PLUNDER

SO TRAPPED PERSON IF YOU ARE HEAR

DONT BE AFRAID THERE IS NO ONE HERE

THAT HATES YOUR LIFE AND HATES YOUR BEING

YOUR LIFE IS HERE YOUR LIFE IM FREEING

LITTLE BOY

LITTLE BOY CAN YOU NOT TELL

WHAT LIFE IS LIKE INSIDE YOUR CELL

THERE'S NO ONE HERE TO TELL A LIE

THERE'S NO ONE HERE TO MAKE YOU CRY

FOR WE ARE BROTHER'S TRAPPED WITHIN

AND WE ARE JOINED AND WE ARE KIN

DO COME RIGHT OUT AND SEE THE LIGHT

IT'S GOOD OUT HERE SO CLEAND AND BRIGHT

I KNOW YOUR HURT I KNOW YOU'RE SCARED

BUT THERE'S SO MUCH THAT CAN BE SHARED

AND THEN ONE DAY WE BOTH SHALL MEET

AND ON THAT DAY WILL BE A TREAT

FOR LONG ENOUGH YOUVE BEEN TRAPPED THERE

THE WAIT IS OVER FOR I DO CARE

IT'S TIME FOR YOU TO SHOW YOURSELF

TO CLAIM YOUR LIFE AND BE YOURSELF

WHY

WHY CANRN'T YOU FEEL WHY CARN'T YOU SEE

THE BITTERNESS YOU CAUSED IN ME

WHAT IS THIS THING THAT MAKES YOU CRUEL

THEN YOU TREET ME LIKE A FOOL

IM NOT A FOOL I NEVER WAS

I KNEW NO BETTER JUST BECAUSE

YOU MADE ME FEEL A LITTLE LESS

AND MADE ME FEEL AN AWFUL MESS

BUT NOW IM BACK AND YOU WILL SEE

THE PERSON I HAVE MADE OF ME

BUT I DONT CARE AND YOU DONT COUNT

IM FINISHED NOW YOU'RE BOWING OUT

YOU NEVER SAW YOU NEVER CARED

ALL MY THINGS YOU NEVER SHARED

ALL THE THINGS THAT I WOULD DO

WERE NEVER GOOD ENOUGH FOR YOU

SO I AM WINNING AND YOU'LL SEE

THAT ALL MY LIFE BELONGS TO ME

<u>*LEVEL TWO*</u>

FROM THE DEPTH I HAVE RISEN

FROM THE DARK AND LONLEY PRISON

TO THE LEVEL THAT I FIND

IVE LEFT THE DARKNESS FAR BEHIND

THE JOURNEY NEXT I HAVE TO FIND

MYSELF AND ME I LEFT BEHIND

UPTO THE NEXT LEVEL TWO

WHERE I CAN SEE THE LIGHT SHINE THROUGH

<u>LOST CHILDREN</u>

CHILDREN LOST CHILDREN FOUND

ALL OUR DREAMS LAY UNDERGROUND

BEING THERE FOR ALL THESE YEARS

WOEFULL LIVES AND WOEFULL TEARS

MAKING ALL OUR LIVES REGRESS

BLAMING IT ON NIGHT TIME STRESS

BUT ALL THE TIME WE KEEP IT HIDDEN

BECAUSE WE THOUGHT IT WAS FORBIDDEN

NOW IT'S COMING TO THE TOP

AND ONE DAY OUT IT WILL POP

TO LOVE TO CRY TO FEAR TO HATE

ALL THE TIME WE SHUT THE GATE

TO ALL THE ONES WE LOVE AND CHERISH

AND HOUR BY HOUR THE LOVE WE PERISH

UNTIL WE FIND THE REASON WHY

OUR LIFE IS LIVED UPON A LIE

THE DREAMS WE THOUGHT LIFE WILL DIE

IF WE COULD ONLY ONCE BUT TRY

TO GET THE TRUTH OUT IN THE OPEN

THEN WE CAN SAY WE ARE TRULY COPING

<u>LOST LITTLE BOY</u>

LITTLE BOY LOST LITTLE BOY FOUND

LIVING IN A WORLD SO PROFOUND

IT IS HEAVEN IS IT HELL

WHO CAN KNOW AND WHO CAN TELL

WE WERE BORN ON MOTHER EARTH

TO GIVE OUR ALL TO GIVE OUR WORTH

WHO KNOWS WHERE IT ALL WILL END

IT MAY EVEN SEND YOU ROUND THE BEND

WE ONE DAY MAY FIND WE WERNT SO BLIND

TO GIVE IT ALL TO MANKIND

TO GIVE OUR ALL TO GIVE OUR WORTH

AND TO ONE DAY LIVE ON MOTHER EARTH

ANOTHER NIGHT ANOTHER DREAM

NEVER KNOWING WHAT IT MEANS

IS IT TRUTH IS IT FORBIDDEN

ALWAYS THERE ALWAYS HIDDEN

CONSTRICTING LIFE CONSTRICTING THOUGHT

NEVER KNOWING NEVER TAUGHT

IS IT EVIL IT IS TRUE

NEVER KNOWING TILL IT COMES THROUGH

<u>**AFRAID AND HELPLESS**</u>

AFRAID AND HELPLESS TRAPPED INSIDE

I CAN NOT SEE I ONLY HIDE

I DONT KNOW WHY THIS FEELING IS HERE

I DONT KNOW WHAT I TRULY FEAR

UNDERGROUND EMOTIONS REELING

TOTAL TRAUMA TOTAL FEELINGS

IM TRAPPED INSIDE THIS LONELY CELL

I CAN NOT SPEAK I CAN NOT TELL

FOR THE REASON I AM HERE

NO ONE WILL TELL NO ONE WILL HEAR

FOR FILLS THIS LONELY PRISON

WHAT CAN I DO TO MAKE ME RISEN

AND FLY AWAY TO PARTS ANEW

AND GET THE HELL AWAY FROM YOU

PHYSICAL PAIN I KNOW I FEEL

EMOTIONAL PAIN IS SOMETHING REAL

BUT I WILL FIND A WAY TO RUN

AND BE THE MAN I HAVE BECOME

AND PAIN AND TRUTH AND LIES GO REELING

SO I CAN HAVE A BETTER FEELING

FORGIVENESS

FORGIVENESS COMES FROM LETTING GO

THE NEED TO MAKE THEM SUFFER

FORGIVENESS COMES FROM LETTING GO

AND LEAVE IT TO THE OTHERS

FOR WHAT THEY HAVE DONE TO ME

I WOULD LIKE THEM TO SUFFER

BUT I DONT CARE AND THEY DONT MATTER

I HAVE LEFT IT TO THE WINDS TO SCATTER

I HELD A GRUDGE FOR MANY YEARS

AND I HAVE SPILLED SO MANY TEARS

BUT NOW I LIVE MY LIFE FOR ME

YOU ARE GONE AND I AM FREE

FOR EVERY ROAD HAS ITS TURNING

AND THE TRUTH I AM LEARNING

SO GO YOU NOW FOR I FORGIVE

AND LEAVE ME TO MY LIFE TO LIVE

TANGLED WEB

WHAT TANGLED WEB TO WE WEAVE

AND OURSELVES DO WE DECIEVE

THE THINGS THAT ARE TAUGHT

THE THINGS WE ARE TOLD

WHEN WE ARE YOUNG AND WHEN WE ARE OLD

AND ALL OUT DREAMS WE LEAVE BEHIND

BECAUSE NO ONE WAS EVER KIND

AND ALL THIS TIME WE LIVE IN STRIFE

ANDTHIS IS NOT THE KIND OF LIFE

WE WISHED FOR US AND WHISHED TO BE

AND LEFT BEHIND OUR HOPES AND DREAMS

AND THEN REPLACED BY BITTER SCREAMS

AND IN OUR HEART THIS DREAM FORGOT

AND TRULY THINK THIS IS OUR LOT

BUT DONT YOU FRET AND DONT YOU STEW

FOR ONE DAY YOUR LIGHT WILL SHINE THROUGH

THE TIME IS RIPE THE TIME IS NOW

FOR US TO TAKE OUT THAT UNUSED PLOUGH

AND REAP AND SOW OUR DREAMS TO GROW

AND TO THE WORLD OURSELVES WILL SHOW

<u>***LOST SOULS***</u>

*THE LOST SOULS OF CHILDREN ARE HEARD
THROUGHOUT THE LAND*

*BUT NO ONE GIVES A DAMB AND NO ONE LENDS A
HAND*

BUT WHAT IF THIS CHILD WAS REALLY YOU

WHAT WOULD YOU SAY WHAT THINGS WOULD YOU DO

BUT YOU HAVE NEVER BEEN IN THIS PLACE

AND PROBABLY NEVER WILL

*SO HOW CAN YOU FEEL AND KNOW WHAT MAKES ME
ILL*

SO GIVE A THOUGHT TO AL LTHE KIDS

WHO NEVER HAD NO ONE

SO TELL THE TRUTH AND YOU WILL SEE

YOU LIFE WILL BE WELL DONE

PIECES OF MY LIFE KEEP COMING TO THE TOP

PIECES OF MY LIFE THEY NEVER STOP

BUT WHEN THE PIECES COME TOGETHER

WHEN IT IS OVER AND DONE

THE PIECES WON'T BE PIECES THEN AND MY LIFE WILL BE AS ONE

<u>SO FAR</u>

I HAVE COME SO FAR YET NOT FAR ENOUGH

I HAVE BEEN THROUGH THICK AND THIN

THROUGH SMOOTH AND ROUGH

THE DISTANCE I HAVE TRAVELED SEEMS SO VERY LONG

YET IT IS NOT QUIET OVER AND I HAVE TO BE STRONG

THE JOURNEY NOT YET TRAVELED MAYBE LONG MAYBE TRYING

BUT I HAVE GOT TO REACH MY GOAL BEFORE I END UP DYING

AS I LOOK BACK ON MY LIFEAT ALL THE PAIN IVE TAKEN

AND ALL THE TIMES FORSAKEN

TO THE CROSSROADS OF MY LIFE AND NOTHING ELSE SHOULD MATTER

AND TO TAKE ALL THESE FEARS I FEEL AND MAKE THEM ALL JUST SCATTER

THEN I WILL BE BORN ANEW AND SPEND MY LIFE JUST LOVING YOU

<u>THE ANGEL</u>

AND ANGEL CAME TO ME ONE NIGHT

AN ANGEL GOOD AND TRUE

AN ANGEL CAME TO ME ONE NIGHT

THIS THING I SAY TO YOU

I JUST LAY THERE MEZMERISED AND NEVER SAID A
WORD

SHE TOLD ME THINGS ABOUT MY SELF

THINGS I HAVE NEVER HEARD

SHE TOLD ME OF MY HOPES AND DREAMS THAT I HAVE
YET TO DO

SHE TOLD ME THINGS ABOUT MY LIFE

THESE THINGS I SAY TO YOU

AND TOLD ME THINGS ABOUT MY LIFE

OF THINGS IVE YET TO SEE

AND SAID ALL I HAVE TO DO IS REALLY JUST BE ME

ONE DAY YOU WILL FIND A GREAT BIG STAR

AS STAR TO GUIDE YOU HOME

THEN YOU WILL TRULY FIND YOURSELF

AND NEVER BE ALONE

THE WAY

THE WAY IS LOST I KNOW NOT WHY

ALL THE TIMES I REALLY TRY

BUT NOONE COME TO TELL ME WHY

AND NO ONE TELLS ME WHY I CRY

IF THE TRUTH MUST TELL AND IT MAY HURT

I WANT TO KNOW SO DONT BE CURT

I FIND THE WAY SO I MAY SEE

AND REALLY KNOW WHAT IS IN ME

AND REALLY KNOW WHAT' HIDDEN THERE

I WANT TO KNOW FOR I DONT CARE

SO SHOW ME HOW THE TRUTH TO SEE

THEN I CAN LIVE AND I CAN BE FREE

<u>MAYBE</u>

IF YOU LOOK INSIDE YOUR HEART

YOU MAY SEE WHAT'S REALLY THERE

AND MAYBE YOU MAY THINK A BIT

AND SOMETIME YOU MAY CARE

AND MAYBE YOU MAY REALISE THAT YOU'R NOT STUFF

YOU MAY THINK YOUR MIND IS ALL FULL OF STUFF

AND MAYBE IF YOU STOPPED ONE DAY

AND MAYBE IF YOU'R KIND

AND MAYBE IF YOU STOPPED ONE DAY

AND MAYBE IF YOU'R KIND

THE WORLD WOULD BE BETTER PLACE

AND MAYBE YOU MAY FIND

THAT ALL THE THINGS YOU WISH IN LIFE

DONT REALLY MEAN A LOT

SO THEN YOU WOULD BE SATISFIED

AND NEVER LOSE THE PLOT

<u>PROTECTOR</u>

PLEASE PROTECTOR IF YOUR THERE

DONT YOU WORRY DONT DESPAIR

THE PERSON YOU PROTECT YOU SEE

FOR THAT PERSON IS REALLY ME

IF YOU LET ME SHARE WITH YOU

THEN MY LIFE WON'T BE SO BLUE

LET ME FIND THE DOOR TO LIFE

AFTER ALL MY WOUNDS AND STRIFE

DONT YOU THINK I DO DESERVE

TO SEE THE MASTER THAT I SERVE

LET ME IN DONT LOCK ME OUT

EVEN THOUGH I CRY AND SHOUT

I WONT HURT HIM FOR YOU SEE

THAT PERSON THERE IS REALLY ME

<u>**THINGS WE HOPE**</u>

WHAT THINGS WE HOPE WITH THINGS WE FIND

FOR ALL OUR DREAMS WE LEFT BEHIND

FOR ALL THE HOPES THAT WE FORGOT

AND ALL THE PAST THAT WE HAVE NOT

AND MAYBE ONE DAY WE WILL LEARN

TO GIVE SOMETHING IN RETURN

AND ALL THE LOVE THAT WE HAVE LOST

AND SOMEDAY WILL COUNT THE COST

OF LIVING RIGHT AND LIVING FREE

WILL ONE DAY COME TO YOU AND ME

UNTIL THAT DAY WE WILL SEARCH

AND LEAVE BEHIND THE PAIN AND HURT

AND TRUTH WILL MANIFEST IN ME

EVEN THOUGH I WON'T BE FREE

BUT ONE DAY THE TRUTH WILL HIGHTEN

THEY THAT DAY YOU WON'T BE FRIGHTENED

<u>COATS OF MANY COLOURS</u>

*COATS OF MANY COLOURS THAT WE SHOW TO THE
WORLD*

COATS OF MANY COLOURS ON A BOY OR A GIRL

*ALL OUR FEELING THAT WE HIDE INSIDE THESE MANY
COATS*

*TO HELP US GET THROUGH THE DAY TO US REALLY
COPE*

*AND ALL THE TIME WE KID OURSELVES THE FEELING
ARN'T TRUE*

*NEVER SHOWING TO THE WORLD THE FEELING THAT
COME THROUGH*

*WE PUT THEM ON ONE BY ONE WHEN WE ARE HURT OR
SCARED*

*BECAUSE THE WORLD IS HURTING US AND WE ARE NOT
PREPARED*

*FOR WE ARE DIFFERANT CHILDREN SEE AND WE ARE
NOT LIKE YOU*

*FOR WE CANNOT SHOW OUR FEELINGS THE PERSON
THAT IS TRUE*

BUT WE WILL TAKE THEM OFF ONE DAY

THESE COATS THAT WE ALL WEAR

*TO MAKE OUR WORLD TO MAKE OUR DREAMS TO MAKE
OUR LIVE PREPARE*

<u>**FALSE OR REAL**</u>

WHAT DO WE KNOW WHAT'S FALSE OR REAL

WHY DO WE FEEL THE WAY WE FEEL

WHAT MAKES US THINK THAT WE POSSES

THE RIGHT TO STRUGGLE AND TO STRESS

DO ANIMALS FEEL THE WAY WE FELL

CAN THEY KNOW IF IT IS REAL

I THINK THEY DO FOR I HAVE FOUND

THE THINGS THEY DO ARE QUIET PROFOUND

THEY LISTEN TO THE WORDS WE SAY

THE ANSWER IS A BARK OR A NIEGH

SO WE SHOULD LEARN FROM WHAT THEY SAY

BUT WE DONT BARK AND WE DONT NIEGH

WE TALK IN WORDS THAT DO COME OUT

BUT NOT IN ANGER NOT IN SHOUT

SO SOFT AND QUIET SO WE DONT SCARE

THE PEOPLE FOR WHOM WE CARE

FOR IF WE DONT CARE FOR PEOPLE WE CHERISH

EVERYTHING WE DO WILL DIE AND PERISH

LIFE

FOR ALL OUR LIVES

FOR ALL OUR DREAMS

WHAT LIVES WE HAVE LIVED

AND LIVES WE HAVE NOT

NOW LIFE IS A GAME

WE PLAY FROM THE START

AND ALL OF THE PAIN WE KEEP IN OUR HEART

TODAY IS A LIFE THAT WE HAVE FORGOT

WHAT PAIN IS HERE AND WHAT PAIN IS NOT

TO WHICH OUR FATHERS BETROTHED IN THEIR WILLS

FOR LIVES ENTRENCHED IN DREAMS

AND DREAMS WE FORFILLED

FOR WHERE ARE THE HERO'S WE LIVE UPTO

AND WHERE ARE THE PEOPLE THAT ARE NOT UNTRUE

SO SWEAT HOW YOU MUST AND LIVE IN YOUR HEART

FOR I AM HERE AND NEVER WILL PART

LOCKED INSIDE

I FOUND I WAS A CHILD LOCKED INSIDE A MAN

I HIT OUT AT EVERYONE AS OFTEN AS I CAN

NO ONE EVER FOUND AND NO ONE EVER SAW

MY FEARS AND HOPES AND DREAMS LOCKED IN LIKE A CLAW

BUT NOW I HAVE FOUND A BETTER WAY

TO MAKE MY LIFE FORFILLED

AND TRY TO REDEEM MYSELF

FOR THE LOVE I HAVE KILLED

THE JOURNEY I NOW UNDERTAKE

AND THE BITTER I NOW FORSAKE

BUT I HAVE BECOME A BETTER MAN

AND I WILL DO ALL I CAN

TO SET THIS CHILD WITHIN ME FREE

THEN THE MAN WILL A LAST BE FREE

<u>FACE THE TRUTH</u>

NOW IS THE TIME TO FACE THE TRUTH

NOW IS THE TIME TO FIND THE PROOF

FOR ALL MY SENSES TO UNITE

TO GET RID OF THIS DREADFUL FRIGHT

BEHIND THE DOOR THE TRUTH IS THERE

AND ALL I DO IS TAKE THE DARE

TO OPEN UP THE DOOR AND SEE

WHAT THE HELLS BEEN SCARING ME

IM AT THE POINT OF NO RETURN

AND I DONT THINK IN HELL I'LL BURN

IT'S A FEAR IVE CARRIED LONG

TO FIND OUT WHAT IS TRULY WRONG

PERHAPS THE ANSWER LIES IN ME

BUT I WAS ALWAYS TO BLIND TO SEE

AND ALL THE HURT AND ALL THE WRONG

THAT I HAVE CARRIED FOR FAR TOO LONG

BUT WHAT'S THIS HURT AND WHAT'S THIS DREAD

IS IT REALLY IN MY HEAD

OR WAS I GIVEN ALL THIS STRIFE

FOR ME TO CARRY ALL MY LIFE

SO WHEN IM THERE PLEASE PRAY FOR ME

AND HELP ME FIND THE TRUTH TO SEE

AND ALL THIS HURT AND ALL THIS PAIN

WILL FINALY NOT BE IN VAIN

THE STORY

WHEN THE STORY HAS BEEN TOLD

AND THE TRUTHS THE DO UNFOLD

WILL YOU SIT THERE IN YOUR CHAIR

AND IN YOUR EYES THE WORLD TO STARE

OR WILL YOU GET UP OFF YOUR BUM

AND DO THE THINGS YOU SHOULD HAVE DONE

AND DONT PUT BLAME ON OTHER FOLKS

BECAUSE YOU THINK THAT LIFES A JOKE

AND GO AND GET THE THINGS YOUR AFTER

AND FILL YOUR LIFE WITH FUN AND LAUGHTER

WE MORTALS LIVE FOR A SHORT TIME

DO DONT LET HATRED MAKE YOU BLIND

AND MAKE THIS LIFE THAT YOU HAVE LEFT

AND LEAVE THIS WORLD WITH JUST YOUR GIFT

AND THEN THE ONES THAT DO COME AFTER

KNEW THAT YOU WERE FUN AND LAUGHTER

<u>MEN FROM MARS</u>

DO YOU KNOW THAT MEN FROM MARS

DONT RIDE BIKES AND DONT DRIVE CARS

THEY HAVE LITTLE WHEELS UPON THIER FEET

MAKES THEM MOBILE MAKES THEM NEAT

THEY ALL GAZE DOWN UPON THIS PLACE

FIGURING THE HUMAN RACE

THEY WON'T CONTACT THEY WON'T SHOW

FOR THE TRUTH THEY REALLY KNOW

FOR OF THEY DID THEIR FUTURE'S BLEAK

FOR WE WOULD MAKE THEM INTO FREAKS

WE HAVE NOT LEARNED FOR TO SHARE

WITH SOMEONE WHO LIVES OUT THERE

WE HAVE NOT GOT THINGS RIGHT ON EARTH

FROM THE ONSET OF OUR BIRTH

<u>THINGS WE HAVE DONE</u>

THINGS WEVE BEEN

THINGS WEVE SEEN

THINGS WEVE HAD

AND THINGS WEVE BEEN

COWBOY'S INDIAN'S MEN FROM MARS

UNDER THE SUN AND UNDER THE STARS

CHILDHOOD MEMORIES LONG FORGOTTEN

WAS IT GOOD OR WAS IT ROTTEN

MEMORIES ONCE ONE DAY MAY RETURN

BUT I DONT KNOW COURSE ITS FORGOTTEN

WAS I GOOD WAS I BAD

WAS I CHEERIE WAS I SAD

A LONG LOST CHILDHOOD NOMEMORY FOUND

HIDDEN DEEP AND UNDERGROUND

WILL IT EVER TO RETURN

AND FROM THE ANSWERES I WILL LEARN

MY PLIGHT

UNTIL YOU UNDERSTAND MY PLIGHT

YOU CAN NOT UNDERSTAND MY FIGHT

THOUGH IT SEEMS THAT I DONT CARE

AND ALL THE THOUGHTS THAT I DONT SHARE

I DONT KNOW WHERE I AM GOING

SO THESE THINGS THAT I AM NOT KNOWING

SO THE THINGS THAT I CAN NOT SHARE

WITH THE ONES THAT REALLY CARE

IF YOU ARE STRONG AND NEVER FAULTER

ALL THESE THINGS I AM BOUND TO ALTER

AND ALL MY TRUTHS AND MY FEAR

ONE DAY WILL MAKE IT ALL TO CLEAR

SO DONT BE MORNFULL AND DONT YOU JUDGE

AND DONT YOU EVEN BEAR A GRUDGE

I CAN NOT HELP THE WAY I AM FEELING

SOMETIMES MY MIND IS FOREVER REELING

AND IF YOU HELP ME MAKE IT THROUGH

THEN TO MYSELF I WILL BE TRUE

THE GLASS MAN

WHERE ARE YOU TAKING ME MY LITTLE GLASS MAN

I THOUGHT I HAD GONE AS FAR AS I CAN

BUT NOW YOU HAVE SHOWN ME A DIFFERNT ROAD

AND ONLY LISTENED AND THEN I WAS TOLD

TO LOOK DEEP INSIDE TO LEVEL TWO

AND MAYBE THE TRUTH WILL FINALLY COME THROUGH

BUT I HAVE NOT TO WORRY AND I HAVE NOT TO GRIEVE

IF NOT LEVEL TO MAYBE THREE

I AM GETTING CLOSER TO WHAT I FEAR MOST

MAYBE IS NOT FEAR MAYBE A GHOST

A GHOST FROM MY PAST I HAVE BURIED DEEP

THAT COMES OUT TO HAUNT ME WHEN I AM ASLEEP

I MUST FIND THE ANSWER AND FEAR NOT TO TREAD

THEN I WILL SLEEP SOUNDLY AND SAFE IN MY BED

<u>**ALL THIS**</u>

LIVES LAY BLEEDING TORN AND TATERED

NEVER KNOWING WHAT REALY MATTERED

ALL THE TIMES OUR LIVES REGRESS

NEVER KNOWING HOW TO ADDRESS

AND ALL THE TIME WE THINK WE ARE WHOLE

AND THE THINGS THAT WE HAVE BEEN TOLD

BUT I KNOW DIFFERENT FOR I HAVE FOUND

THINGS THAT HAVE LAYED UNDERGROUND

AND ALL THIS TIME I BLAMED MYSELF

FOR THINGS IVE DONE AND THINGS IVE FELT

BUT NOW IT IS REALLY TURNING AROUND

AND I WONT BE LEFT HANGING AROUND

FOR SELF ASTEEM IS WHAT I CRAVE

AND I AM NOT GOING TO MY GRAVE

WITH BITTERNESS AND DREAMS NOT FOUND

FOR I WILL MAKE IT ALL TURN AROUND

<u>FOR TIMES</u>

FOR TIMES WE REMEBER

FOR TIMES WE HAVE BEEN TOLD

FOR TIMES GONE BY

FOR TIMES WE GROW OLD

NOW TIME IS THE ENEMY

FOR PEOPLE IN STRIFE

AND ALL OF THE THINGS THAT HAPPEN IN LIFE

NOW IF YOU LIVE RIGHT

BY THE THINGS YOU HAVE BEEN TAUGHT

AND ALL OF THE THING YOU HAVE SERCHED FOR

AND THINGS THAT YOU HAVE SOUGHT

AND WHEN YOU HAVE GONE TO THIS PLACE IN YOUR HEART

AND DONT SEEM SO PERFECT

AND DONT SEEM SO RIGHT

DONT BLAME OTHERS AND DONT BLAME YOURSELF

YOU JUST LIVE RIGHT AND LOOK AFTER YOURSELF

THE TRUTH

PONDER PONDER WILD AND WONDER

WHAT MAKES THE LIGHTNING RAIN AND THUNDER

THEY ITS GOD THEY SAY ITS WEATHER

THE MAKES THE GRASS THE FLOWERS AND HEATHER

THE WHERE THE WHY THE RYME AND REASON

THE CHANGES THE TIME WORLDS AND SEASONS

THE LITTE CHILD THAT GROWS UP KNOWING

HE IS DIFFERNT BECAUSE IT'S SHOWING

ASK THE TRUTH BUT NO ONE KNOWS

THEY ONLY KID THAT ALSO SHOWS

THEN HE WILL FIND IT IN HIS PAST

THEN HE WILL BE FREE AT LAST

<u>**DREAMS**</u>

WHAT EVER DREAMS WE CARE TO HAVE

WHAT EVER DREAMS WE CARE TO NOT

WHAT EVER DREAMS WE CARE TO HOLD

WHAT EVER DREAMS THAT DO UNFOLD

AND IN OUR DREAMS WHAT THOUGHTS DO SPING

AND IN OUR HEARTS WHAT BELLS DO RING

UNTIL WE NEVER DREAM AT ALL

INTO OUR SLEEP OUR MINDS DO FALL

UNTIL WE WAKE INTO THE FEAR

AND THINGS AND THOUGHTS THAT JUMP AND REAR

AND TAKE OUR MINDS BACK TO OUR YOUTH

THE FIND WHAT LIES INSIDE THE TRUTH

BUT TRUTH IS NEVER EASILY SOUGHT

INSIDE OUR BODIES MIND AND THOUGHT

BUT ONE DAY WE MAY EASILY FIND

THE TRUTH THAT LIES WITHIN OUR MIND

AND BRING US BACK WHERE WE BELONG

THE DAYS ARE NEAR AND WONT BE LONG

IT

SILLY THOUGHTS RUN THROUGH MY HEAD

FROM GETTING UP TO GOING TO BED

SILLY THOUGHT YOU WOULD SAY IM ODD

AND SAY TO ME YOU SILLY SOD

BUT THEY ARE THOUGHTS SILLY AS THEY MAY SEEM

IT MAYBE A NIGHTMARE IT MAYBE A DREAM

BIT IF I GET TO THE BOTTOM OF IT

I CAN PONDER AND WONDER AND MAYBE SIT

IF I CAN GET TO THE BOTTOM OF IT

AND GET RID OF ALL THIS HASSLE

MY HOME ONE DAY MAY BECOME MY CASTLE

<u>LOVE</u>

WHAT IS THIS THING WE CALL LOVE

THAT MAKES US ALL RISE ABOVE

YOU CAN NOT BUY IT YOU CAN NOT CLAIM IT

BUT YOU CAN SURELY DRAIN IT

IT'S IN YOUR HEART AND IN YOUR SOUL

ITS EVEN THERE WHEN WE GROW OLD

WHAT'S THE THING THAT WE ALL CHERISH

AND THIS THING WE EASILY PERISH

WE ARE MOTRAL IT IS TRUE

HUMAN BEINGS THROUGH AND THROUGH

WITH HOPES AND WANTS AND EVEN DREAMS

FOR CARS AND BOATS AND EVEN SCREAMS

BUT THIS THING WE TRULY CHERISH

AND WE HOPE WILL NEVER PERISH

ALL THESE THINGS WE WILL RISE ABOVE

IF WE HAVE THIS THING CALLED LOVE

<u>REALLY ME</u>

JUST YOU WAIT TILL GET YOU OUT

AND OF THAT THERE IS NOT DOUBT

I KNOW ITS DARK I KNOW ITS DISMAL

AND AT TIME CAN BE ABISMAL

BUT STAY RIGHT THERE FOR I AM COMING

FAST AS I CAN FAST AS IM RUNNING

THEN TOGETHER WE WILL BE

THEN AT LAST WE WILL BE FREE

ALL THE LIES THAT KEPT YOU HIDDEN

FOR ALL THE THINGS YOU WERN'T FORGIVEN

IT'S ALL COMING TO AN END

JUST COME RIGHT OUT AND BE MY FRIEND

ALL THIS TIME YOU HAVE BEEN ALONE

ALL THIS TIME YOUVE HAD NO HOME

JUST YOU WAIT AND YOU WILL SEE

ALL YOU ARE IS REALLY ME

<u>TEARS</u>

FOR ALL THE LIVES FOR ALL THE TEARS

FOR ALL THE BITTER BITTER YEARS

WHAT IS LIFE WE HAVE FORGOT

FOR ALL THE DREAMS WE HAVE FORGOT

TO DREAM TO HAVE TO HOPE TO FEAR

FOR WE TO SHED THE LONLEY TEAR

AND THE BABES NOT YET BORN

AND ALL THE LIVES WE HAVE TO SCORN

FOR TO HOPE FOR LIVES TO BEAR

AND ALL THE TIMES WE ALL SHALL SHARE

WHAT IS THE THING WE HAVE FORSAKEN

AND ALL THE LIVES TURNED TO SATAN

BUT YOU WILL FIND A LOVES THAT'S THERE

A LOVE SO STRONG A LOVE SO RARE

AND SOMEDAY WHEN YOUR LIVES TURNED ROUND

AND YOU GET CLOSER TO THE GROUND

MAYBE THEN YOU WILL SEE WHAT'S REAL

AND THE TRUTH YOU REALLY FEEL

AND ALL THE THINGS THAT YOU CARN'T SEE

FOR THEN YOU'LL KNOW IT'S REALLY ME

<u>THE TRUTH IS OUT THERE</u>

I CANNOT FALL I CANNOT RISE

TO SEE THE THINGS BEFORE MY EYES

I RUN I CRAWL BUT CANNOT SEE

THIS THING THAT QUELLS IN SIDE OFME

FOR I WAS GETTING FAR TO CLOSE

THE TRUTH WAS NEAR FOR ME TO TOAST

BUT NOW IT'S GONE I DONT KNOW WHERE

I LOOK INSIDE BUT ONLY STARE

THERE IS NOTHING THERE I CANNOT SEE

WHY HAVE YOU DONE THIS THING TO ME

IF I WAS CLOSE AND YOU WERE THERE

WHY DONT YOU SHARE THIS THING WITH ME

FOR I AM NOT SCARED OF WHAT COME OUT

THE FEAR HAS GONE THERE IS NO DOUBT

SO SHOW YOURSELF FOR ME TO SEE

AND MAKE THIS PERSON WHOLE AND FREE

IVE LOST THE WAY I CANNOT FIND

IVE LOST THE THOUGHTS INSIDE MY MIND

SO IF IT'S TRUTH YOU ARE ALL ABOUT

THEN SHOW YOURSELF AND COME RIGHT OUT

FAME AND FORTUNE

FAME AND FORTUNE IS SOME PEOPLES DREAM

BUT FAME AND FORTUNE'S NOT EVERYONES SCENE

IF YOU LOOK AROUND YOU AT THINGS YOU HAVE GOT

INSTEAD OF WONDERING AT THINGS YOU HAVE NOT

IF YOU LOVE THE THINGS YOU CHERISH

YOU'RE HOPE AND DREAMS WILL NEVER PERISH

IF YOU LOOK AROUND YOU WILL SEE

MATERIAL THINGS ARE NOT FOR THEE

FOR IF YOU LOVE SOMEONE YOU CARE

AND YOUR LIFE WITH THEM YOU SHARE

ALL YOUR HOPES WILL COME TO YOU

AND TO YOURSELF YOU WILL BE TRUE

FOR THE TRUTH THAT I WILL SEE

MATERIAL THINGS ARE NOT FOR ME

FOR I HAVE LIVED FOR MANY YEARS

FULL OF HATE AND FULL OF FEARS

TRYING TO BE WHAT I AM NOT

TRYING TO GET THE THINGS IVE GOT

BUT THEY DONT MATTER AND YOU WILL FIND

YOU HAVE TO LIVE AND BE SO KIND

AND HELP THE WORLD TO FIND ITS PLACE

AND BE A PART OF THE HUMAN RACE

<u>*TIME*</u>

TIME IS AND ENEMY

TIME IS A FRIEND

TIME IS A STORY

THE PLOT NEVER ENDS

BUT TIME IS SOMETHING

WE HAVE ALL GOT

TIME IS A MYSTERY

THAT HAS NOT PLOT

BUT WHEN YOU THINK

WHAT TIME WE HAVE SPENT

TRYING TO FIND WHAT DREAMS HAVE BEEN SENT

AND MAYBE IN TIME OUR LIVES WILL ALLOW

THE PAIN AND SUFFERING WE SHOW ON OUR BROW

AND PERHAPS IN OUR DREAMS THE FEAR MAY NOT RISE

AND FEAR WILL BE REPLACED

BY HAPPENESS IN OUR EYES

<u>**FEAR IN USE**</u>

FOUR SCORE AND TWENTY

IVE LIVED WITH THIS FEAR

FOUR SCORE AND TWENTY

YEAR AFTER YEAR

AND LIFE IS NOT SOMETHING FOR GRANTED WE TAKE

AND SOMETHING FOR SOMEONE TO CRUSH FOR THIER
SAKE

BUT WHAT DO WE DO WHEN NOTHING ALLOWS

AND NOTHING IS GIVEN NOT EVEN A VOW

TO HELP YOU TO GROW AND MAKE YOU LESS FEARED

WHEN YOU WERE FIRST BORN AND THEN YOU WERE
REARED

AND WHAT DID THEY TAKE THAT MADE YOU THIS WAY

FOR FEAR IS THE PERSON WHO'S WITH YOU EACH DAY

FOR NOW IS THE TIME AND NOW IS THE WAY

ANDMAYBE THE ANSWERE LIES WITH US TODAY

<u>YOU NEVER CAME</u>

I HAVE NO SISTERS OR BROTHER TOO

YOU HAVE SOMEONE TO COMFORT YOU

I HAD NO ONE WITH GOOD INTENT

BECAUSE I HAD AND ACCIDENT

NO ONE WOULD LISTEN TO MY PLEA

NO ONE CAME TO COMFORT ME

A LITTLE BOY THAT LOST HIS WAY

ALL YOU SAID WAS GO OUT AND PLAY

YOU NEVER SAW THE HURT IN ME

YOU NEVER LISTENED TO MY PLEA

YOU JUST LIED AND MADE ME SEE

YOU NEVER CAME TO COMFORT ME

ALL THE LIES AND ALL THE TEARS

AND ALL THE BITTER BITTER YEARS

WHY DONT YOU LOOK WHY DONT YOU SEE

BUT ALL YOU DO IS LOOK THROUGH ME

YOU NEVER SAW THE HURT IN ME

YOU NEVER LISTENED TO MY PLEA

YOU JUST LIED AND MADE ME SEE

YOU NEVER CAME TO COMFORT ME

SO WHAT'S MY LIFE BUT JUST A LIE

I JUST HANG MY HEAD AND CRY

FOR YOUTH THAT'S LOST AND LOVE NOT GIVEN

AND THE THAT'S NOT YET RISEN

I KNOW YOU HURT

I KNOW YOU HURT I KNOW YOU CRY

AND EVERYDAY YOU WANT TO DIE

BUT DONT YOU LIVE THIS LIFE THAT'S GIVEN

FOR ALL YOU SINS CAN BE FORGIVEN

AND START ANEW WITH PASSION AND PRIDE

AND ALL YOU PAINS WILL THEN SUBSIDE

YOU'RE THOUGHT AND FEELINGS ARE YOUR OWN

AND BETTER SEEDS THERE WILL BE SOWN

AND GROW TO BE A BETTER MAN

I KNOW YOU WILL AND KNOW YOU CAN

*YOUVE COME THROUGH WORSE WITH COLOURS
FLYING*

SO DONT STOP NOW JUST KEEP ON TRYING

FOR YOU WILL FIND THE LIGHT ABOVE

FULL OF HOPE AND FULL OF LOVE

SO DONT YOU WAIT THE TIME HAS COME

FOR YOU TO COME BACK TO THE ONE

WHO NEEDS YOU NOW AND RIGHTLY SO

AND THEN THE TWO OF US CAN GROW

<u>**PROTECTOR**</u>

OH PROTECTOR PLEASE DONT STRAY

I JUST WANT FOR YOU TO STAY

YOU MAY THINK YOUR JOB IS DONE

AND YOU TREAT HIM LIKE YOUR SON

HE'S THE THING INSIDE MY MIND

AND THE TRUTH I HAVE TO FIND

SO YOU CAN LET HIM BE FREE

THEN YOU CAN PROTECT ME

I CANNOT SEE I CANNOT HEAR

I CANNOT TOUCH I ONLY FEAR

WHAT IS THIS THING THAT MAKES ME SCARED

I ONLY KNOW I COME PREPARED

TO MEET MY SOUL TO MAKE ME CARE

I KNOW ITS DARD INSIDE THIS LAIR

BUT MAYBE NOW YOU KNOW I CARE

FOR YOUR TRUST I HAVE TO WIN

YOU MUST KNOW I AM YOUR KIN

PROTECTOR SHOW HIM THE WAY

BUT DONT YOU GO YOU HAVE TO STAY

THE JOB YOU HAVE DONE FOR ALL THESE YEARS

PROTECTING ME FROM HURT AND TEARS

IT'S OVER NOW SO PLEASE COME OUT

THE TRUTH IS HERE THERE IS NO DOUBT

THINGS

WHAT THINGS WE HOPE WHAT THINGS WE FIND

FOR ALL THE DREAMS WE LEFT BEHIND

AND ALL THE HOPES THAT WE FORGOT

ADN ALL THE PAST THAT WE HAVE NOT

AND ONE DAY WE MAY LEARN

TO GIVE SOMETHING BACK IN RETURN

AND ALL THE LOVE THAT WE HAVE LOST

AND MAY SOMEDAY COUNT THE COST

OF LIVING RIGHT AND LIVING FREE

WILL ONE DAY COME TO YOU AND ME

UNTIL THAT DAY WE WILL SEARCH

AND LEAVE BEHING THIS PAIN AND HURT

AND THINGS WILL MANEFEST IN ME

EVEN THOUGH WE ARE NOT FREE

BUT SOMEDAY SOON THE TRUTH WIIL HIGHTEN

AND ON THAT DAY WE WONT BE FRIGHTENED

THE GIFT

I HAVE THIS GIFT INSIDE OF ME

IVE KEPT IT THERE NO ONE TO SEE

BUT ONE DAY I'LL FIND IT THERE

AND THEN THE WORLD WITH IT I'LL SHARE

AND THAT DAY IS SOON TO COME

MY HEART WILL RISE AND SO THE SUN

UNTIL THAT DAY I'LL TRY MY HARDEST

TO FIND A WAY AND REAP THE HARVEST

ALL THESE THINGS IVE LOCKED INSIDE

ALL MY HOPES AND ALL MY PRIDE

THE FLOOD GATES SOON ARE GOING TO OPEN

A TRUER WORD WAS NEVER SPOKEN

<u>**THINGS**</u>

FOR ALL THE THINGS THAT WE HAVE GOT

FOR ALL THE THINGS THAT WE FORGOT

ARE THEY STILL THERE ARE THEY STILL REAL

FOR ALL THE THINGS WE TOUCH AND FEEL

I HAVE THIS DREAM THAT NO ONE SHARES

BECAUSE WE FEEL NO ONE CARES

CAN NO ONE SEE THE HURT WITHIN

CAN NO ONE SEE WHERE I HAVE BEEN

I LOVE I CRY I HURT I DIE

WHEN I AM FED UP I EVEN SIGH

CARN'T YOU COME OUT AND LET ME SEE

THE LITTLE BOY THAT'S ONLY ME

IF YOU DO THIS THING AND LET ME SEE

YOU WILL BE FREE AND SO SHALL ME

<u>COATS</u>

COATS OF LIFE WE SHOW TO OTHERS

COATS OF LIFE OURSELVES TO SMOTHER

ONE BY ONE WE PUT THEM ON

ONE BY ONE BY ONE BY ONE

UNTIL OUR FEAR AND ALL OUR HOPES

ARE HIDDEN DEEP INSIDE OUR COATS

NEVER SHOWING TO THE WORLD OUTSIDE

WE WEAR THESE COATS WITH LOVING PRIDE

AND THEN ONE DAY WE ALL FIND OUT

WHAT THESE COATS ARE ALL ABOUT

BUT WE HAVE TO CLIMB INSIDE

AND FIND OUT WHERE WE LEFT OUR PRIDE

AND ONE BY ONE BY ONE BY ONE

THESE COATS WILL COME OFF ONE BY ONE

AND FIND OUT WHERE OUR PATH MAY LEAD

EVEN THOUGH ARE HEARTS MAY BLEED

THE TRUTH IS THERE FOR US TO FIND

THEN WE ALL WONT BE SO BLIND

AND ALL THE DAYS WE HAVE LEFT HERE

WILL MAKE OUR LIVES OH SO DEAR

THE MEANING OF LIFE

I HAVE FOUND THE MEANING

THE MEANING OF LIFE

I HAVE FOUND THE MEANING

THROUGH TROUBLE AND STRIFE

I DONT KNOW WHERE IT IS LEADING

PERHAPS I'LL NEVER KNOW

BUT I HAVE GOT TO GO THERE

THIS PLACE I HAVE TO GO

DO IF YOU FIND ME WONDERING

WHAT LIFE IS ALL ABOUT

YOU CAN JOIN ME IN MY QUEST

AND MAYBE YOU WILL FIND OUT

I DONT KNOW WHAT LIES AHEAD

FOR I HAVE HAD PAIN INSIDE MY HEAD

MAYBE ITS ALL FOR GOOD

MAYBE ITS ALL FOR BAD

MAYBE ITS ALL FOR HAPPINESS

MAYBE ITS ALL FOR SAD

BUT I WILL KEEP ON GOING

NO MATTER HOW LONG IT TAKES

AND THEN THE ANSWER I WILL FIND

MAKING LIFE A TRUER KIND

<u>SCORN</u>

WHAT HAVE I DONE FOR ALL THIS SCORN

ARE YOU SORRY I WAS BORN

WHAT HAVE I DONE FOR ALL THIS HATE

AND ALL MY LOVE YOU DISSAPATE

WHAT IS THIS THING THAT YOU KEEP HIDDEN

AND THE HATE THAT KEEPS YOU DRIVEN

YOU ARE OLD AND SOON WILL DIE

TAKING WITH YOU THIS ONE LIE

WHAT IS SO BAD YOU CARN'T FORGIVE

AND GIVE ME BACK MY LIFE TO LIVE

YOU CHOSE YOUR LIFE OF HURT AND LIES

NEVER WANTING FOR TO RISE

MY LIFE IS MINE NOT YOURS TO TAKE

SO JUST GET RID OF ALL YOUR HATE

AND GIVE ME BACK MY LIFE TO LIVE

AND THEN TO SOMEONE'S LOVE I'LL GIVE

DARKNESS INSIDE

FOR OURSELVES WE DO DECIEVE

FOR OURSELVES WE DON'T BELIEVE

HIDDEN THOUGHTS AND HIDDEN DREAMS

HIDDEN SHOUTS AND HIDDEN SCREAMS

NEVER KNOWING DAY BY DAY

WHY WE REALLY ARE THIS WAY

PERHAPS ONE DAY AROUND I'LL TURN

THEN THESE THOUGHTS I'LL REALY SPURN

THEN THE LIGHT WILL THEN SHINE THROUGH

THEN TO MYSELF I WILL BE TRUE

WE HAVE NO REASON TO TAKE FLIGHT

WHAT GIVES ME WORRY WHAT GIVES ME FRIGHT

WHAT MAKES ME THINK I CAN NOT COPE

I LOSE ALL REASON I LOSE ALL HOPE

OF ALL THE THINGS I TRY TO HIDE

THAT CAUSES TURMOIL ALL INSIDE

WHAT HOPE HAVE I TO LIVE A LIFE

FREE OF WORRY FREE OF STRIFE

WHAT IS THIS THING I CANNOT FACE

THE THING THAT'S HIDDEN IN ITS PLACE

DOWN INSIDE MY SOUL IT HIDES

DOWN DEEP INSIDE THE THING RESIDES

NOT EVER COMING TO THE LIGHT

PERHAPS LIKE ME IT'S FULL OF FRIGHT

LOST CHILD

CHILDREN LOST CHILDREN FOUND

ALL OUR DREAMS LAY UNDERGROUND

BEING THERE FOR ALL THESE YEARS

WOEFULL LIVES AND WOEFULL TEARS

MAKING ALL OUR LIVES REGRESS

BLAMING IT ALL ON DAYTIME STRESS

BUT ALL THE TIME WE KEEP IT HIDDEN

BECAUSE WE THOUGHT IT WAS FORBIDDEN

NOW IT'S COMING OUT ON TOP

AND ONE DAY OUT IT SOON WILL POP

ALL OUR DREAMS WE KEEP WELL HIDDEN

BECAUSE WE THOUGHT

IT WAS FORBIDDEN

TO LOVE TO CRY TO FEAR TO HATE

ALL THE TIME WE SHUT THE GATE

TO ALL THE ONES WE LOVE AND CHERISH

AND HOUR BY HOUR THE LOVE WE PERISH

UNTIIL WE FIND THE REASON WHY

OUR LIFE IS LIVED UPON A LIE

THE DREAMS THE THOUGHTS THE LIFE WILL DIE

IF ONLY ONCE WE COULD TRY

TO GET THE TRUTH OUT IN THE OPEN

THEN WE CAN SAY WERE TRULY COPING

<u>INSIDE OF ME</u>

WHAT IS THIS THING INSIDE OF ME

THAT I CAN NOT SEE BUT I CAN FEEL

THAT MAKES ME FALL THAT MAKES ME RISE

THAT TORMENT THAT DWELLS INSIDE

I TRY TO FIGHT I TRY TO RISE

IT'S ALWAYS THERE WHEN I CLOSE MY EYES

PLEASE GO AWAY AND LET ME BE

THEN AT LAST I WILL BE FREE

I CAN NOT SEE I CAN NOT TELL

I CAN NOT SEE INSIDE THIS HELL

I CAN NOT TELL I CAN NOT CRY

IS THE TRUTH OR JUST A LIE

FOR ALL THE BITTENESS GONE BY

WHAT HOPE OF I WHO CAN NOT CRY

WHAT CHANCE HAVE I THAT CAN NOT GIVE

WHAT CHANCE I HAVE WHO CAN NOT LIVE

TO SLEEP TO DREAM AND THEN TO FEAR

EXPLANTIONS THAT JUST NOT CLEAR

IM JUST A CHILD THAT'S LOCKED AWAY

I JUST WANT TO GO OUT AND PLAY

FOR ALL THE REASONS RIGHT OR WRONG

IVE BEEN LOCKED HERE FOR FAR TO LONG

SO COME AND GET ME OUT SOME DAY

THEN I CAN GO OUT AND PLAY

HUMANS CAN NOT FLY

I ONCE MET A MAN ONE DAY

WHO TOLD ME HE COULD FLY

WHY HE REALLY TOLD ME THIS

I REALLY DON'T KNOW WHY

HE SAID HE FLEW DOWN TO BRAZIL

THE WEATHER WAS SO BLEAK

IT TOOK TWO DAYS TO GET THERE

TO FLY BACK TOOK A WEEK

THEN HE FLEW TO PISA

TO GAZE UPON THE TOWER

BEING SO CLOSE TO US

ONLY TOOK AN HOUR

HE ONLY FLEW IN DAYLIGHT

BUT TRIED IT IN THE DARK

AND LANDED IN THE OCEAN

AND WAS EATEN BY A SHARK

THE MORAL OF THIS STORY

IS HUMANS CAN NOT FLY

SO KEEP YOUR FEET ON THE GROUND

IT'S FOOLISH JUST TO TRY

DARKNESS RESIDES

I WANT THIS THING I HAVE TO PASS

I WANT TO KICK IT IN THE ARSE

IVE HAD IT FOR TO LONG YOU SEE

THE DARKNESS THAT'S INSIDE OF ME

TO PLUCK IT OUT FROM WHERE IT HIDES

WHERE IT IS HIDDEN WHERE IT RESIDES

ALL THE TRUTH THEN I WILL SEE

WHAT THE FEAR IS INSIDE OF ME

WHY DO I ALWAYS STAND AND WAIT

WHY CAN I NOT OPEN UP THE GATE

TO FIND OUT WHAT IT IS I HATE

TO GO RIGHT IN AND NOT PROCRASTINATE

SO NOW I HAVE TO MAKE A STAND

AND OFFER OUT A LOVING HAND

THEN ALL MY FEAR AND ALL THE DREAD

AND ALL THE THOUGHTS INSIDE MY HEAD

WILL ONE DAY SPREAD THIER WINGS AND FLY

AND THEN MY LIFE WON'T BE A LIE

NOW IS THE TIME FOR ME TO FIGHT

TO GET IT OUT AND NOT TAKE FLIGHT

TO FACE THIS HORROR THAT'S WITHIN

SO I CAN START ALL OVER AGAIN

I HAVE TO FREE WHAT I AM YEARNING

TO MAKE MYSELF WHOLE TO MAKE MYSELF FREE

IT TAKES TIME IT TAKES COURAGE

SO I MUST NOT BE DISCOURAGED

TO WHERE ANGELS FEAR TO TREAD

TO FACE THE HURT TO FACE THE DREAD

LONELY GIRL

THERE IS THIS LONELY GIRL

WHO SITS ALONE AND CRIES

MANY PEOPLE SEE HER

MANY PEOPLE PASS HER BY

IN THIS WORLD OF MANY

WHY SHOULD SHE BE ALONE

IN THIS WORLD OF PLENTY

WHY HAS SHE GOT NO HOME

THERE IS THIS LONELY GIRL

WHO SITS ALONE AND CRIES

WHY DO WE NOT REACH OUT TO HER

AND GIVE HER ALL OUR LOVE

JUST LIKE WE WERE PROMISED

BY THE GOD ABOVE

MAYBE IF WE JUST REACH OUT

HER LONELY TEARS WILL DRY

AND MAYBE IF OUR LOVE IS STRONG

AND MAYBE IF WE TRY

THIS LONELY GIRL WON'T BE ALONE

HER LONELY HEART WON'T DIE

THERE IS THIS LONELY GIRL

WHO SITS ALONE AND CRIES

IT'S DARK IN THERE

JUST WAIT THERE ILL GET YOU OUT

AND OF THAT THERE IS NO DOUBT

I KNOW ITS DARK I KNOW ITS DISMAL

AND AT TIMES IT'S SO ABISSMAL

BUT STAY RIGHT THERE BECAUSE IM COMING

FAST AS I CAN FAST AS IM RUNNING

THEN TOGETHER WE WILL BE

THEN AT LAST WE WILL BE FREE

ALL THE LIES THAT KEPT YOU HIDDEN

FOR THE THINGS YOU WERE NOT FORGIVEN

IT'S ALL COMING TO AND END

JUST COME OUT AND BE MY FRIEND

ALL THIS TIME YOUV'E BEEN ALONE

ALL THE TIME YOUV'E HAD NO HOME

JUST WAIT THERE AND YOU WILL SEE

ALL YOU ARE IS REALLY ME.

<u>**TOMMY TURPIN**</u>

LITTLE TOMMY TURPIN

A BOY FROM OUT OF TOWN

ONCE CAME TO THE CITY

TO HAVE A LOOK AROUND

HE MARVELLED AT THE BUILDINGS

THE TRAFFIC AND THE STREETS

HE WALKED AROUND FOR HOURS

AND NOW HE HAD SORE FEET

HE SAT DOWN ON A BENCH

IN THE PRETTY PARK

AND THEN HE SLOWLY FELL ASLEEP

AND WOKE UP IN THE DARK

NOW FOR A COUNTRY BOY

IN THE CITY AFTER DARK

IT WASN'T SUCH A GOOD IDEA

IT WASN'T SUCH A LARK

A LADY OF THE NIGHT

WENT PASSING BY THE BENCH

AND SAID TO OUR YOUNG TOMMY

WOULD YOU LIKE TO TRY A WHENCH

NOW TOMMY DID NOT UNDERSTAND

AND RAN AWAY IN FRIGHT

AND VOWED TO RETURN HOME

THE VERY SAME NIGHT

NOW THE MORAL OF THIS STORY

IS VERY PLAIN TO SEE

THAT IF YOU LIVE IN THE COUNTRY

THE CITY'S NOT FOR THEE

<u>THE BIRD</u>

A VISION CAME TO ME ONE NIGHT

IN THE SHAPE OF A MIGHTY BIRD

HE TOLD ME THINGS ABOUT MYSELF

THAT I HAVE NEVER HEARD

HE TOLD ME OF THINGS AND PLACES

THAT I HAVE NEVER SEEN

I JUST SAT THERE MESMERISED

AND NEVER SAID A WORD

BEING IN THE PRESENCE

OF THIS MIGHTY BIRD

I GAZED INTO HIS GREAT BIG EYES

HIS EYES SO FULL OF POWER

BUT HE JUST KEPT ON TALKING

HOUR AFTER HOUR

HE SAID IF WE JUST TRUST OURSELVES

THE TRUTH WE'LL ALWAYS FIND

AND IF WE ARE SO LOVING

SO GENTLE AND SO KIND

SO IF YOU THINK THAT LIFES UNFAIR

AND YOU DON'T REALLY HAVE A CARE

ALL YOU DO IS LOOK AROUND

AT THINGS THAT WE ALL SHARE

TURNER

WE HAVE THIS DOG CALLED TURNER

AS BIG AS HE COULD BE

HE HAS THESE QUEEN ANN BACK LEGS

FOR ALL THE WORLD TO SEE

HE LOOKS JUST LIKE A BALLERINA

WHEN HE HAS A PEE

DOING THE PAR DE DUR

FOR ALL THE CROWD TO SEE

WHEN WE TAKE HIM FOR A WALK

HE TRULY THROWS A WOBBLY

IF WE DIDN'T GET HIM THROUGH THE DOOR

HE'D DO IT IN THE LOBBY

WHEN HE EATS HIS DINNER

IT'S AS IF HE STARVED FOR WEEKS

HE GOBBLES DOWN HIS DINNER

AND JUST FILLS UP HIS CHEEKS

AND IF YOU SAW HIM STOOD THERE

YOU WOULD SAY MY GOD

BUT DON'T YOU BE AFRAID

CAUSE HE'S A REAL SOFT SOD

MORRISON

WE HAVE THIS GREAT BIG PUSSY CAT

MORRISON IS HIS NAME

NOW HE HIS GETTING OLDER

HE'S BECOMING JUST A PAIN

HE ALWAYS CRIES TO GO OUT

THEN CRIES TO COME ON IN

THEN CRIES TO GO OUT

AND CRIES TO COME IN AGAIN

ALL HE DOES IS SIT THERE

ALL HE DOES IS EAT

WE HAVE COME TO THE CONCLUSION

HE HAS HOLLOW FEET

NOW WHAT DO YOU DO WITH A CAT

YOU HAVE HAD FOR YEARS

IT WOULD BE CRUEL

TO BURY HIM UPTO HIS EARS

BUT HOW DO YOU GET SOME SLEEP

THROUGH THE LONG LONG NIGHT

CAUSE WE HAVE GOT THIS PUSSY

WHO DOESN'T GIVE SHITTE

GETTING YOU OUT

JUST WAIT THERE I WILL GET YOU OUT

AND OF THAT THERE IS NO DOUBT

I KNOW ITS DARK I KNOW ITS DISMAL

AND AT TIMES IT IS ABISMAL

BUT STAY RIGHT THERE BECAUSE IM COMING

FAST AS I CAN FAST AS IM RUNNING

THEN TOGETHER WE WILL BE ME

THEN AT LAST WE WILL BE FREE

ALL THE LIES THAT KEPT YOU HIDDEN

FOR ALL THE THINGS YOU WERE NOT FORGIVEN

IT'S ALL COMING TO AN END

JUST COME OUT AND BE MY FREIND

ALL THIS TIME YOU HAVE BEEN ALONE

ALL THIS TIME YOU HAD NO HOME

JUST WAIT THERE AND YOU WILL SEE

ALL YOU ARE IS REALLY ME

<u>*INSIDE OF ME*</u>

WHAT IS THIS THING INSIDE OF ME

THAT I CAN NOT SEE BUT I CAN FEEL

THAT MAKES ME FALL THAT MAKES ME RISE

THAT TORMENT THAT DWELLS INSIDE

I TRY TO FIGHT I TRY TO RISE

IT'S ALWAYS THERE WHEN I CLOSE MY EYES

PLEASE GO AWAY AND LET ME BE

THEN AT LAST I WILL BE FREE

I CAN NOT SEE I CAN NOT TELL

I CAN NOT SEE INSIDE THIS HELL

I CAN NOT TELL I CAN NOT CRY

IS THE TRUTH OR JUST A LIE

FOR ALL THE BITTENESS GONE BY

WHAT HOPE OF I WHO CAN NOT CRY

WHAT CHANCE HAVE I THAT CAN NOT GIVE

WHAT CHANCE I HAVE WHO CAN NOT LIVE

TO SLEEP TO DREAM AND THEN TO FEAR

EXPLANTIONS THAT JUST NOT CLEAR

IM JUST A CHILD THAT'S LOCKED AWAY

I JUST WANT TO GO OUT AND PLAY

FOR ALL THE REASONS RIGHT OR WRONG

IVE BEEN LOCKED HERE FOR FAR TO LONG

SO COME AND GET ME OUT SOME DAY

THEN I CAN GO OUT AND PLAY

<u>SEASONS COME</u>

SEASONS COME AND SEASONS GO

ITS DARK IN HERE SO I DONT KNOW

IF WRONG IS WRONG AND RIGHT IS RIGHT

WHY DONT YOU LISTEN TO MY PLIGHT

PLEASE FREE ME FROM WHERE I AM KEPT

AND THEN THE TRUTH I WILL EXCEPT

BUT I AM HERE INSIDE THIS PLACE

AND YOU HAVE NEVER SEEN MY FACE

BUT WAIT ONE DAY I WILL BE THERE

AND ALL OUR LIFE WE WILL BOTH SHARE

I JUST HOPE IT'S NOT TO LATE

FOR YOU TO OPEN UP THE GATE

I AM TRAPPED WITHIN YOUR SOUL

AND ALL I WANT IS TO BE WHOLE

SO TRY YOUR BEST I KNOW YOU CAN

AND FREE ME FROM THE PLACE I AM

<u>LIES AND BITTER YEARS</u>

FOR ALL THE LIES FOR ALL THE TEARS

FOR ALL THE BITTER BITTER YEARS

WHAT IS THIS LIFE WE HAVE FORGOT

AND ALL THE DREAMS THAT WE HAVE NOT

TO DREAM TO HAVE TO HOPE TO FEAR

FOR WE TO SHED THIS LONELY TEAR

AND THE BABIES NOT YET BORN

AND ALL THE TIMES WE ALL WILL SCORN

FOR TO HOPE FOR LIVES TO BEAR

AND ALL THE TIMES WE ALL SHALL SHARE

WHAT IS THIS THING WE HAVE FORSAKEN

AND ALL THE LIVES NOW TURNED TO SATIN

BUT YOU WILL FIND A LOVE THAT'S THERE

A LOVE SO STRONG A LOVE SO RARE

AND SOMEDAY WHEN YOUR LIVES TURN AROUND

AND YOU GET CLOSER TO THE GROUND

MAYBE THEN YOU WILL SEE WHAT REAL

AND THE TRUTH YOU REALLY FEEL

AND ALL THE THING YOU CAN NOT SEE

THEN YOU WILL KNOW IT' S REALLY ME.

DREAMS AND HOPES

WHAT THOUGHTS AND PLEASURES WE DERIVE

JUST FROM MEARLY BEING ALIVE

WHAT DREAMS WHAT HOPES HAVE WE HIDDEN

FOR WANT'S AND POSSESTIONS WE ARE DRIVEN

WHAT OF OUR DREAMS WE HAVE FORGOT

WE THROW ASIDE FOR IT WAS NOT

THE THING TO DO TILL TIME FORGOT

WE HAVE CHOICES THAT I KNOW

THE THINGS WE WANT THE THINGS WE SHOW

BUT NOW'S THE TIME TO MAKE A STAND

AND TAKE THE FUTURE BY THE HAND

WE MUST BELIVE IN WHAT IS RIGHT

AND MAKE THE DARKNESS INTO LIGHT

GO FOR OUR DREAMS AND MAKE THEM HAPPEN

WE HAVE HELD BACK WE HAVE BEEN SLACKIN

NOW IS THE TIME FOR US TO GO

TO OURSELVES WE HAVE TO SHOW

<u>**TIME**</u>

TIME IS AN ENEMY

TIME IS A FRIEND

TIME IS A STORY

THE PLOT NEVER ENDS

BUT TIME IS SOMETHING

WE HAVE ALL GOT

TIME IS A MYSTERY

THAT HAS NO PLOT

BUT WHEN YOU THINK

WHAT TIME YOU HAVE SPENT

TRYING TO FIND OUT

WHAT DREAMS YOU HAVE BEEN SENT

AND MAYBE IN TIME

OUR LIVES WILL ALLOW

THE PAIN AND SUFFERING

WE SHOW ON OUR BROW

AND PERHAPS IN OUR DREAMS

THE FEAR MAYNOT RISE

AND FEAR WILL BE REPLACED

BY HAPPINESS IN OUR LIVES

FOUR SCORE

FOUR SCORE AND TWENTY

IVE LIVED WITH THIS FEAR

FOUR SCORE AND TWENTY

YEAR AFTER YEAR

AND LIFE IS NOT SOMETHING

FOR GRANTED WE TAKE

AND SOMETHING FOR SOMEONE

TO CRUSH FOR THEIR SAKE

BUT WHAT DO WE DO

WHEN NOTHING ALLOWS

AND NOTHING IS GIVEN

NOT EVEN A VOW

TO HELP YOU GROW

AND MAKE YOU LESS FEARED

WHEN YOU WERE FIRST BORN

AND THEN YOU WERE REARED

AND WHAT DID THEY TAKE

TO MAKE YOU THIS WAY

FOR FEAR IS THE PERSON

WHO IS WITH YOU EACH DAY

FOR NOW IS THE TIME

AND NOW IS THE WAY

AND MAYBE THE ANSWER

LIES HERE TODAY

<u>IM NOT BLIND</u>

YOU SHOW ME THINGS THAT I DONT KNOW

YOU TAKE ME PLACES I DONT GO

YOU START TO TELL ME THEN LEAVE ME FLAT

YOU STAY THERE AND I GO BACK

WHAT IS THIS THING YOU TRY TO TELL

AND ALL THE WORDS YOU TRY TO SPELL

TO UNDERSTAND ME I MUST KNOW

TO UNDERSTAND ME I MUST GO

INTO THE PLACE YOUR LEADINGME

TO SHOW ME THINGS I HAVE TO SEE

DONT BE AFRIAD BECAUSE I WON'T CRY

IVE DONE ALL THAT MY EYES ARE DRY

ILL SEE THE TRUTH YOU WILL SHOW

YOU LEAD THE WAY I WANT TO GO

SO TAKE ME THERE WERE I BELONG

FOR I HAVE WAITED FAR TO LONG

WITH YOU BESIDES ME I WON'T FALTER

THE TWO OF US MY LIFE WILL ALTER

THE TRUTH IS THERE FOR US TO FIND

SO TAKE ME THERE FOR IM NOT BLIND

SELDOM

SELDOM DO WE GET THE CHANCE

TO LIVE OUR LIVES AND TO ADVANCE

FOR MANY YEARS I THOUGHT ABOUT OTHERS

MOTHERS FATHERS SISTERS BROTHERS

BUT I AM HERE AND THEY ARE THERE

OUR LIVES MAY CROSS BUT NEVER SHARE

THE GRUDGE I BORE JUST MADE ME ILL

I GOT NO ANSWER JUST A PILL

BUT NOW I KNOW THE ANSWERS THERE

FOR I KNOW AND THEY DONT CARE

THEY LIVE THERE LIVES INSIDE A SHELL

THE TRUTH IS THERE BUT THEY WONT TELL

BUT NOW I KNOW IM TRULY RISEN

FOR THERE FAILINGS IVE FORGIVEN

BUT IF THEY SEE AND THEY WON'T TELL

IVE JUST THREE WORDS GO TO HELL

<u>GEORGE THE GOOSE</u>

A GOOSE CALLED GEORGE WOKE UP ONE DAY

AND FOUND HE COULD NOT FLY

NO MATTER HOW HE DID IT

OR HOW MUCH HE TRIED

GEORGE CAME TO THE CONCLUSION

THAT HE COULD NOT FLY

NOW ALL THE REST FLEW SOUTH

TO FRANCE AND ONTO RIO

BUT GEORGE HAD TO BE CONTENT

AND STAY WITH A PIG NAMED CLEO

NOW CHRISTMAS CAME AS IT ALWAYS DID

NO TURKEY COULD BE FOUND

SO FARMER JONES SAID WHY NOT GOOSE

IT'S GOT TO BE TEN POUND

THE FARMYARD TELEGRAPH WAS RIFE

WITH POOR OLD GEORGE'S QUICK DEMISE

SO CLEO SAID TO GEORGE ONE DAY

YOU'D BETTER RUN AND HIDE

FOR FARMER JONES HAS NOTHING

TO FEED HIS BLOOMING LOT

AND CLEO SAID TO GEORGE

YOU FOR THE COOKING POT

SO GEORGE HID UNDER ALL THE HAY

TO WAIT THERE FOR HIS FATE

WHEN HE HEARD OLD FARMER JONES

COMING THROUGH THE GATE

BUT HE WAS KIND OF CARELESS

AND FELL INSIDE THE GATE

AND WHEN HE LANDED ON THE GROUND

THE AXE FELL ON HIS HEAD

THE AXE IT OPENED UP A WOUND

THE BLOOD IT TRICKELED OUT

HE COULD NOT OPEN UP HIS MOUTH

FOR HELP HE COULD NOT SHOUT

SO GEORGE CREPT OUT FROM INSIDE THE SHED

THE SCENE IT CAUGHT HIS GASE

HE HAD TO RUN BACK TO THE HOUSE

THE ALARM HE HAD TO RAISE

HE SAVED THE LIFE OF FARMER JONES

THIS VOW HE DID DECIDE

THAT GEORGE WOULD LIVE HIS LIFE OUT

UNTIL THE DAY HE DIED.

<u>FEARFUL DREAD</u>

YESTERDAY I FELT SAD INSIDE

MY FEAR MY TRAUMA I CAN NOT HIDE

I NEED TO GO INSIDE MY SOUL

TO MAKE ME FILLED TO MAKE ME WHOLE

I FELT REJECTED, NEGLECTED AND STUPID

I NEED A PERSON WITH THE ARROW OF CUPID

TO PIERCE THE DARKNESS I FEEL INSIDE

NO LONGER FOR MY FEARS TO HIDE

WHAT DO I WANT WHAT DO I FEAR

TO ME IT IS NOT REALLY CLEAR

WHY I RUN AND HIDE AND FEAR

I CAN NOT TELL I CAN NOT HEAR

LAST NIGHT AS I LAY INSIDE MY BED

ALL THE THOUGHTS RAN THROUGH MY HEAD

WHAT IS THE THING THAT IS WELL HIDDEN

TO MAKE ME SAD TO MAKE ME DRIVEN

THAT CAUSES ALL THIS FEARFULL DREAD

THIS PAIN AND TORTURE IN MY HEAD

THIS DEMON THAT I CAN NOT TOUCH

THAT IS STILL USING ME FOR A CRUTCH

ONE DAY I HOPE I WILL DRIVE IT OUT

THEN I WILL BE ABLE TO SHOUT

GLORY BE TODAY IM FREE

<u>STUCK FOR WORDS</u>

WHAT LOOKS YOU GIVE WHAT WORDS YOU UTTER

WHEN YOU FIND I HAVE A STUTTER

YOU LOOK AT ME AS IF I'M CURSED

YOU LOOK AT ME AND EVEN WORSE

YOU THINK IM DAFT YOU THINK IM LOONY

YOU THINK IVE JUST COME FROM THE MOONY

WHY DO YOU LAUGH WHY CARN'T YOU SEE

THE PERSON THAT'S INSIDE OF ME

I LOVE I LAUGH I HURT I CRY

ONE DAY LIKE YOU I'LL EVEN DIE

DON'T YOU THINK I DESERVE A CHANCE

TO GROW TO LIVE AND TO ADVANCE

WHY CARN'T YOU UNDERSTAND IN ME

FOR I AM HERE FOR ALL TO SEE

BUT YOU KEEP ME LOCKED INSIDE MY PRISON

AND MY SOUL HAS NEVER RISEN

TO THE HIEGHTS THAT YOU FEEL

FULL OF LIFE AND FULL OF ZEAL

I HAVE THIS TROUBLE WITH MY TALKING

BUT YOU STAND THIER BLOODY GAULKING

IT'S NOT CONTAGIOUS YOU WON'T CATCH IT

ON THE SURFACE YOU WON'T SCRATCH IT

SO WHEN THE REASON I DO TALK

ALL YOU DO IS STAND AND GAULK

IT'S JUST ME THAT'S STANDING THERE

SO WHY THE LOOKS AND WHY THE STARE

I'M JUST HUMAN AS YOU SEE

I DID NOT CHOOSE IT, IT CHOSE ME

SO STOP THE WAY YOU'RE TREATING ME

IM JUST LIKE YOU AS YOU CAN SEE

<u>**YOU'RE SON**</u>

WHY DON'T YOU SEE WHAT I HAVE DONE

AFTER ALL I'M STILL YOUR SON

WHAT IS THIS THING THAT YOU HATE

WHY DO YOU ALWAYS CLOSE THE GATE

ALL THE LIES THROUGHOUT THE YEARS

ALL THE UPSET PAIN AND TEARS

WHY CARN'T YOU LOVE ME FOR JUST ME

AND NOT FOR SOMEONE I COULD BE

MY OWN LIFE IS WHAT IVE GOT

THAT'S THE THING THAT YOU FORGOT

IT'S MY OWN LIFE AND INDEED

EVEN IF I DON'T SUCCEED

WHAT IS THIS THING THAT I HAVE DONE

AFTER ALL I'M STILL YOUR SON

ALL THE WORDS THAT YOU HAVE SPOKEN

ALL THE PROMISES YOU HAVE BROKEN

FOR FORTY YEARS IVE HAD THIS PAIN

FOR FORTY YEARS YOU'VE WATCHED ME DRAIN

ALWAYS TELLING ME YOUR LIE

KEEPING IT HIDDEN UNTIL YOU DIE

BUT I DON'T CARE FOR I HAVE RISEN

UP ABOVE YOUR HUMAN PRISON

ALL THESE WORDS I HAVE SPOKEN

SAY GOODBYE THE BONDS ARE BROKEN

<u>*COMFORT*</u>

I HAVE NO SISTERS BROTHERS TOO

YOU HAVE SOMEONE TO COMFORT YOU

I HAD NO ONE WITH GOOD INTENT

BECAUSE I HAD AN ACCIDENT

NO ONE WOULD LISTEN TO MY PLEA

NO ONE CAME TO COMFORT ME

A LITTLE BOY THAT HAD LOST HIS WAY

ALL YOU SAID WAS GO AND PLAY

YOU NEVER SAW THE HURT IN ME

YOU NEVER LISTENED TO MY PLEA

YOU JUST LIED AND MADE ME SEE

YOU NEVER CAME TO COMFORT ME

ALL THE LIES AND ALL THE TEARS

AND ALL THE BITTER BITTER YEARS

WHY DON'T YOU LOOK WHY DON'T YOU SEE

BUT ALL YOU DO IS LOOK THROUGH ME

YOU NEVER SAW THE HURT IN ME

YOU NEVER LISTENED TO MY PLEA

YOU JUST LIED AND MADE ME SEE

YOU NEVER CAME TO COMFORT ME

SO WHATS MY LIFE BUT JUST A LIE

I JUST HANG MY HEAD AND CRY

FOR YOUTH THAT'S LOST AND LOVE THAT'S GIVEN

AND THE LIFE THAT'S NOT YET RISEN

<u>MOTHER EARTH</u>

AS PAGES OF OUR LIVES UNFOLD

WHAT WONDERS DO WE SEE

WE LEAVE THESE THINGS ALONE

FOR OTHER FOLKS TO SEE

OR DO WE RUIN EVERYTHING

WITH GREED AND RAPE AND PLUNDER

ALL THE TIME DOES MOTHER EARTH

EVER WINGE AND WONDER

DOES SHE EVER GIVE US A BILL

FOR THINGS WE TAKE FOR GRANTED

AND THE THINGS GROWING HERE

FOR ALL THE THINGS SHE PLANTED

YOU JUST SAY DON'T YOU FRET

IT ALWAYS WILL BE THERE

BUT DON'T YOU GO KIDDING YOURSELVES

THINGS ARE GETTING RARE

THE FISH THAT SWIM THE BIRDS THAT FLY

THE FOOD WE RELY UPON

DON'T YOU GO ON FOOLING YOURSELVES

ONE DAY IT WILL BE GONE